Little
Science
Stars

Light and Sound

The Best Start in Science

By Clint Twist

ticktock

North American edition copyright © *ticktock* Entertainment Ltd 2009.

First published in North America in 2009 by *ticktock* Media Ltd.,
The Old Sawmill, 103 Goods Station Road, Tunbridge Wells, Kent TN1 2DP, U.K.

ISBN: 978-1-84696-191-5

Printed in China
9 8 7 6 5 4 3 2 1

Picture credits (t=top, b=bottom, c=center, l=left, r=right,
OFC=outside front cover, OBC=outside back cover):

Corbis: 12b, 13t, 18t, 20 all, 22l. Powerstock: 10t, 10b, 17 all, 18b, 21t.
Shutterstock: OFC all, 1 all, 2, 3 all, 4–5 all, 6–7 all, 9b, 10–11b, 11 all, 12t (both),
14 all, 15 all, 16 all, 19 all, 21b, 22b, 22–23 background, 23 all, 24 all, OBC both.
ticktock Media Archive: 8–9, 13b.

Every effort has been made to trace the copyright holders, and we apologize in
advance for any unintentional omissions. We would be pleased to insert the
appropriate acknowledgments in any subsequent edition of this publication.

Contents

Any words appearing in the text in bold, **like this**,
are explained in the Glossary.

Light and sound are all around us every day. Without light and sound, we would not be able to see or hear.

Cock-a-doodle-doo

Bright light

Shouting

Loud noise

Light and **sound** are both types of energy.

Light is energy that we see with our eyes. Sound is energy that we hear with our ears.

Where does light come from?

The main way we get light on **Earth** is from the **Sun**. We call this light **sunlight**.

NEVER look directly at the Sun, even if you are wearing sunglasses, because it can damage your eyes.

Sunlight is very **bright** when there are no **clouds**. Bright light helps us easily see things.

Clouds

Clouds in the sky sometimes block out some of the sunlight.

The clouds make the sunlight **dim**, or less bright. It can be harder to see when the light is dim.

Sunflower

Without sunlight, plants, animals, and people could not survive.

Plants need sunlight to help them grow. They use sunlight to make a special food inside themselves.

Without plants, animals and people could not live. We need plants for food.

Why does it get dark at night?

When there is no light, there is **darkness**.

Sun

There is darkness at night because one half of Earth blocks out the Sun's light from the other half.

Our Earth is a big spinning ball. It takes 24 hours to spin all the way around.

A **day** and a night last 24 hours.

As your part of Earth spins away from the Sun, it gets dark. We call this **night**.

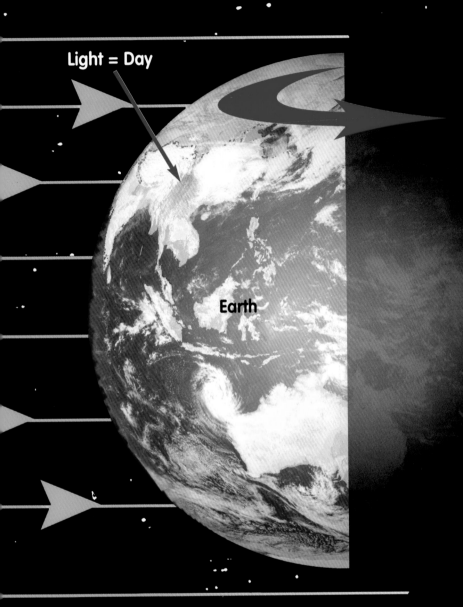

Light = Day

Dark = Night

Earth

When we block the light, it makes the room dark.

There are many ways to block light. We use blinds or curtains to block light at our windows.

Brightest light

Dimmer light

How do we see when it's dark?

When it's dark, we can use **artificial light**.

We can turn on a lamp to make light.

The light is brightest close to the lamp. The light gets dimmer farther away from the lamp.

We can make artificial light by turning on a flashlight, too.

The closer you hold the flashlight to the book, the easier it is to see the words.

At night, drivers turn on their car headlights to light up the road.

At night, we turn on lights in houses, stores, and offices. We use a type of energy called **electricity** to power the lights.

House

Stores

Offices

REMEMBER
Don't waste electricity!
Turn off the light
when you leave a room.

How does light travel?

Light travels in straight lines. This means we cannot see around corners or over walls.

We cannot see who is behind the tree . . .

. . . or what's inside the box.

The dog cannot see the cat because the wall blocks any light traveling between them.

12

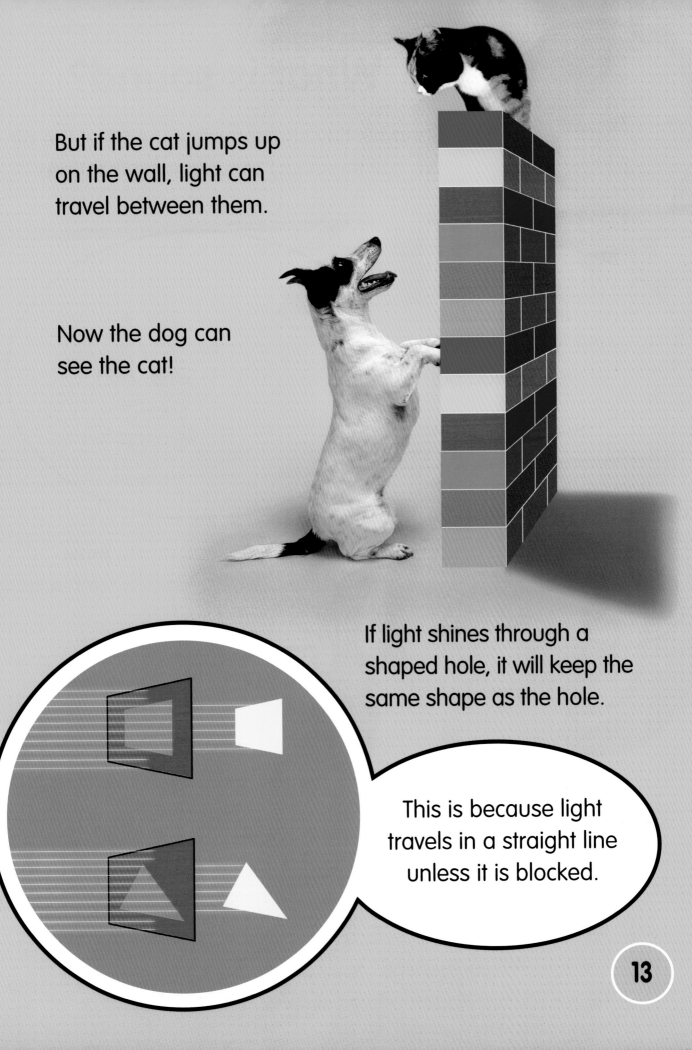

But if the cat jumps up on the wall, light can travel between them.

Now the dog can see the cat!

If light shines through a shaped hole, it will keep the same shape as the hole.

This is because light travels in a straight line unless it is blocked.

What is sound?

Sound is tiny shaking movements of the **air**. We call these tiny movements **vibrations**.

If you drop a pebble into water, you will see little waves spread out.

Waves

Sound vibrations move through the air in the same way.

We cannot feel or see the vibrations, but our ears are designed to detect them.

Our ears pick up the vibrations, and then our brain turns them into sounds that we know.

Ears

An animal's ears work in the same way as your ears.

What makes sounds loud and quiet?

Sounds travel away from the things that made them. As they travel away, they get faint, or quiet.

Drums

The sound of these drums is loud if you are close to them.

If you are far away, the sound is quieter.

We can make loud sounds and quiet sounds.

A whisper is a quiet sound. When we whisper, we can be heard only by people close to us.

Shouting is a loud sound.

We shout when we want someone far away to hear us.

A shout is very loud if you are close to the person who is shouting.

17

How do we make sounds?

This boy is plucking the guitar strings. They vibrate and make sounds that we call music.

Guitar

When the guitar strings stop vibrating, the music stops.

Hitting the top of a drum makes it vibrate and produce sound.

Gently hitting the drum makes a quiet sound. Hitting it hard makes a loud sound.

We can use our voices to make singing sounds.

We can use our hands to make clapping sounds.

Animals make sounds, too.

Hoowwwlllll

Baa Baa

Hello there!

Some parrots learn to make sounds like people!

Can we block out sound?

Sound travels through the air in a different way to light. Sound is not as easy to block as light.

The cat cannot see the dog, but it can hear it barking.

This mother cat cannot see her kitten, but she can hear it meowing.

You can hear this fire engine's siren as it speeds by.

If the fire engine goes around a corner,
you will still be able to hear the siren!

We can stop our ears
from picking up the
sound of the siren by
covering them.

REMEMBER
Don't ever stick
things in
your ears!

Questions and answers

Q Can dogs hear better than people?

A Yes, they can! Dogs can hear sounds that are too quiet for us to hear. They can also hear sounds that are very far away. Dogs can move their ears in different directions to pick up sounds.

Q How many different sounds can you hear in your home or yard?

A Here are some to get you started:
- TV
- Radio
- Vacuum cleaner
- Telephone
- Birds
- Lawn mower

Look around and listen. Some sounds are loud and some are quiet.

Q Can loud noises hurt your ears?

A Yes, they can, so protect your ears. Don't turn the music up too loud if you are wearing headphones.

Q What artificial light did people use before electricity was invented?

A They used candles.

Q How fast do sound vibrations travel through the air?

A They travel at more than 745 miles (1,200km) per hour.

Q What is the fastest thing in the world?

A Light is the fastest thing in our world. Light energy travels in waves at 186,400 miles (300,000km) per hour.

Q What sound in your home can save you from danger?

A A smoke alarm. Make sure a grownup tests the alarm every month.

Glossary

Air A mixture of gases that are all around us on Earth's surface. People and animals breathe air.

Artificial light Light that is made by humans such as through lamps or flashlights.

Bright Easy to see.

Clouds Clusters of water droplets that float in the air.

Darkness When there is no light.

Day The hours when we have daylight from morning to evening.

Dim Difficult to see.

Earth The planet where we live. Earth is a huge ball of rock. It is always spinning.

Electricity A type of energy that we use to make light and heat and to power machines.

Light A type of energy that we see with our eyes.

Night The hours when it is dark from evening to morning.

Sound A type of energy that we hear with our ears.

Sun The Sun is a star, just like the ones we see twinkling in the sky at night. It is closer to Earth than any other star, so we can feel heat from it.

Sunlight Light that comes from the Sun during the day.

Vibrations Tiny movements that happen when something shakes back and forth or from side to side very quickly.

Index